Haiku poems are a style of Japanese poetry expressing a single feeling and embodying three lines of five, seven, and five syllables.

Lovingly dedicated to all seekers. May you be guided by love and return to inner joy.

Follow the author's blog and creative journey on social media @corunumartsy

Love

Love is a fine thing.
When I feel love, I have wings.
Fly little bird, fly.

Patience

Be patient, be calm.
Like gears on a clock that wind,
all good things in time.

Friendship

Sweet and caring smiles,
on faces of precious friends.
Hearts flooding over.

Trust

Little purring cat,
slowly welcoming my arms.
Trust given, trust earned.

Nourishing

Leaves falling from trees,
gently nourshing the land.
Mother Nature's gift.

Peace

Dreaming puppy rests,
feeling cozy, feeling blessed.
Peace begins within.

Playful

Wild dolphins at play,
exploring oceans so deep.
May we be as free.

Loyalty

Oh, our shining moon,
loyally returns each night.
We swoon over you.

Compassion

Feeling compassion,
unending as ocean breeze,
flowing inwardly.

Giving

Sunflowers and bees,
giving, work tirelessly.
As sweet as honey.

Hugs

Hugs are happy things.
When an elephant comes home,
warm greetings received.

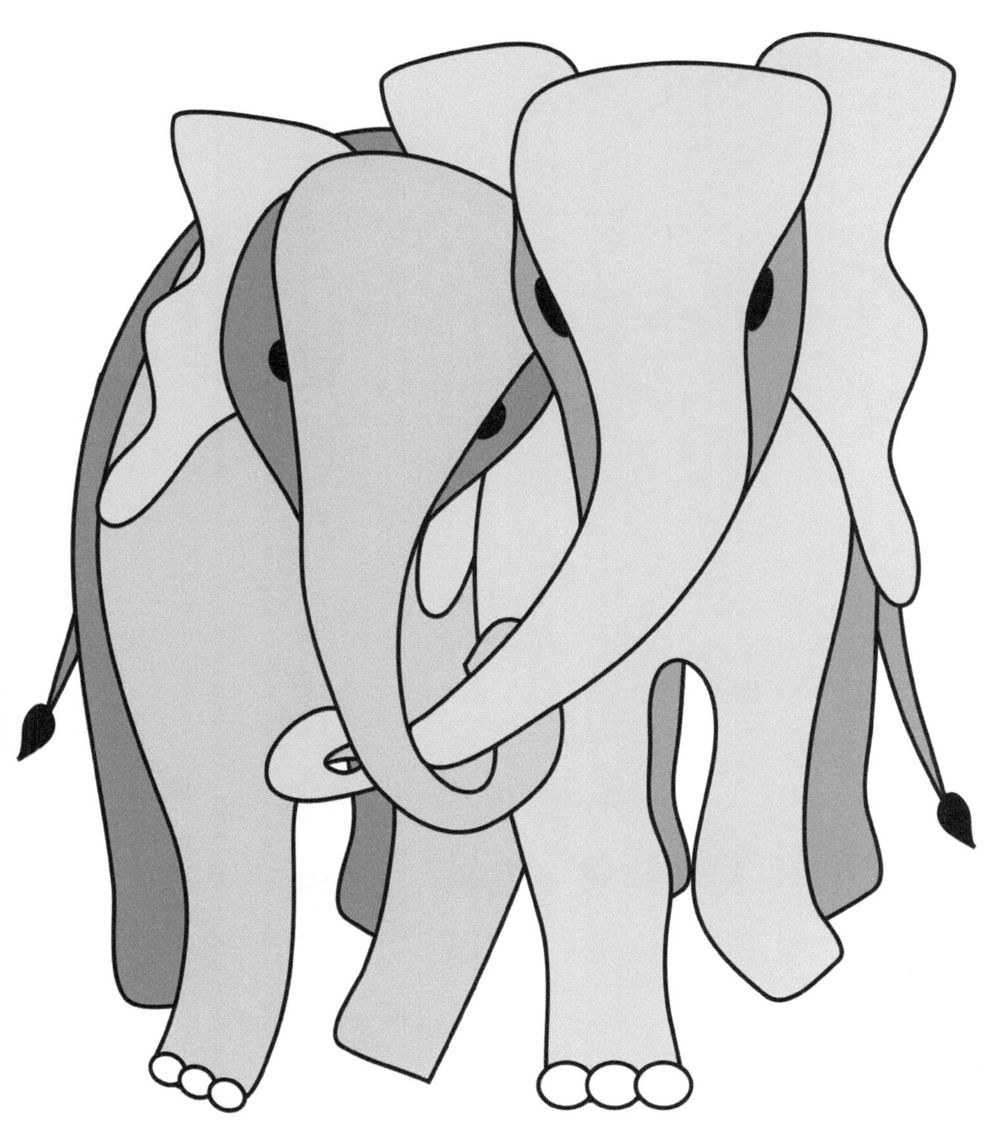

Gratitude

Gratitude is felt,
much like a groomed chimpanzee.
Thanks is shown in love.

Silence

In silence we sit.
Breathing quietly, we wait.
Om beloved, Om.

OMmmmmm
OMmmmmm
OM
OM
OM
OM
OM
OM
OM
OMmmmmm
OMmmmmm
OM
OM

Heather's Happy Haikus
are meant to ignite the divine spark
of joy in each reader.

Write your very own haiku poem here:

5 ________________________________

7 ________________________________

5 ________________________________